Risk Management and ISO 31000

A pocket guide

Risk Management and ISO 31000

A pocket guide

ALAN FIELD

IT Governance Publishing

Every possible effort has been made to ensure that the information contained in this book is accurate at the time of going to press, and the publisher and the author cannot accept responsibility for any errors or omissions, however caused. Any opinions expressed in this book are those of the author, not the publisher. Websites identified are for reference only, not endorsement, and any website visits are at the reader's own risk. No responsibility for loss or damage occasioned to any person acting, or refraining from action, as a result of the material in this publication can be accepted by the publisher or the author.

Apart from any fair dealing for the purposes of research or private study, or criticism or review, as permitted under the Copyright, Designs and Patents Act 1988, this publication may only be reproduced, stored or transmitted, in any form, or by any means, with the prior permission in writing of the publisher or, in the case of reprographic reproduction, in accordance with the terms of licences issued by the Copyright Licensing Agency. Enquiries concerning reproduction outside those terms should be sent to the publisher at the following address:

IT Governance Publishing Ltd
Unit 3, Clive Court
Bartholomew's Walk
Cambridgeshire Business Park
Ely, Cambridgeshire
CB7 4EA
United Kingdom
www.itgovernancepublishing.co.uk

© Alan Field 2023

The author has asserted the rights of the author under the Copyright, Designs and Patents Act, 1988, to be identified as the author of this work.

First published in the United Kingdom in 2023 by IT Governance Publishing.

ISBN 978-1-78778-415-4

ABOUT THE AUTHOR

Alan Field, LL.B (Hons), PgC, MCQI CQP, GIFireE is a Chartered Quality Professional and Member of The Society of Authors.

Alan has particular expertise in auditing and third party assessing Anti-bribery Management Systems (ABMSs) to ISO 37001 and Integrated Management Systems to ISO 9001 and ISO 14001 requirements. Alan has many years' experience with Quality and Integrated Management Systems in the legal, financial, property services and project management sectors in auditing, assessment and gap analysis roles.

ACKNOWLEDGEMENTS

I would like to thank Gary Hibberd for his comments during the production of this book.

CONTENTS

INTRODUCTION

This pocket guide isn't written for experts on risk management or, necessarily, experts on management systems. However, it does assume the importance of risk management to all organisations – big and small – and recognises that not having a formal process to identify, assess and control risk can lead to many issues, including difficulties in implementing management systems based on ISO standards. The ISO 9000 family of standards are process based, and this pocket guide will focus on how this broad approach works in a wider arena than a process focus would normally involve.

The absence of a risk-based approach to management might also lead to opportunities being missed or simply not being exploited to their full potential. Risk management is not just about managing negative or catastrophic events, decisions on competing research and development possibilities is one example of a positive. A risk-based approach to management may reduce unnecessary expense or divert resources to better controls. For example, ISO 27002 provides 'attributes' to controls (identifying control type, operational capabilities, security domains, cybersecurity concepts and information security properties), helping the risk assessor to make more informed decisions about which controls might best respond to a given risk.

To achieve all these in effectively, we may require a management system that understands risks and opportunities in a strategic way in terms of leadership priorities. It might be tempting to look at these requirements as something tactical or operational but the leadership's attitude towards risk and the priorities for dealing with risks will always impact an organisation's attributes.

This pocket guide is intended to be of interest to those whose experience of risk or management systems has always been very sector based. A life spent looking at financial or governance risk could be surprisingly helpful in understanding how different policies and approaches to risk can be developed.

Annex SL is the structure implemented by ISO standards such as ISO 9001 and ISO 27001. Its purpose is to be a platform for these and other ISO's risk-based management system requirements, so that any size of organisation can create better systems across multiple standards by having a common format of clauses and goals. Even if you never intend to implement something like ISO 27001, reading Annex SL is like reading the UK's HSG65 for health and safety management systems; it contains much food for thought.

This pocket guide will often use the terms 'strategic' and 'tactical', and this will mean different things to different organisations. Annex SL assumes that top management and the wider leadership team take a key part in risk policy and decision making, and this is always useful to be aware of when considering the points made in this pocket guide.

The main focus of this pocket guide will be looking at ISO's Annex SL (sometimes referred to as Annex L) and how it requires a risk-based approach to management to be adopted by other international standards in the ISO 9000 family, e.g. ISO 9001:2015 and ISO 27001:2022. Although risk is referred to regularly in these standards, there isn't much of a practical definition of what risks and opportunities actually mean in practice to an individual organisation; as we will see, one advantage of IS0 31000 is that it can inspire the creation of an infrastructure to achieve a risk universe.

This pocket guide will also discuss how risk can be defined within a management system, i.e. what isn't written in international standards about defining risk and the implications of a risk-based approach to management.

This approach means our focus will be on risk management as a process. Any business process can be designed with risk and opportunities in mind; risk management isn't necessarily a separate silo or discipline that sits alongside process design.

Introduction

When discussing risk management, it is only natural to introduce and analyse ISO 31000:2018. ISO refer to this Standard as the *"international best practice regarding risk management, which is widely accepted, generic and open to manage any type of risk."*[1]

ISO 31000 can be used by any type of organisation. Currently, the Standard isn't subject to third-party assessment in the way for example that ISO 9001:2015 or ISO 27001:2022 are. However, there are organisations that offer second-party audit processes based on ISO 31000's principles. Perhaps the most important aspect of ISO 31000 is the way in which it can influence risk management strategy, and this pocket guide will explore how the Standard can be used to benefit an organisation that is implementing an Annex SL standard such as ISO 9001:2015.

But more important than looking at different risk tools and techniques, is the way ISO 31000 can influence the way risk management is implemented within an organisation.

ISO 31000 looks at the distinction between a risk management framework compared to that of a risk management process. One way of considering this is that there is little point in having lots of individual processes to identify and control risk if there isn't a set of strategic policies and leadership actions that define and support these processes. It flows from this that a framework can be influenced by many factors.

One contemporary example would be planning for resilience – be this to respond to COVID-19 or the shift towards remote working. If we treat COVID-19 as a black swan event (and you could argue against this), those organisations that had invested in resilience were able to adapt more quickly than those who hadn't. Understanding risk and continually reviewing how efficient and adaptable to sudden change an organisation's processes could be at short notice, isn't just a matter of

---

[1] *IWA 31:2020, Risk management – Guidelines on using ISO 31000 in management systems, www.iso.org/standard/75812.html*.

efficiency or continual improvement – which it often is – but it allows for some level of preparedness when unplanned events suddenly arise. With the shift to remote working, organisations that already had an element of this in their processes arguably had already taken strategic views of their risk. However, those who didn't, needed to change their view of risk overnight for any kind of remote working. Reading ISO 31000 could help inspire the setting up of a wider range of policies and processes to keep risk under review at a strategic level. This, in turn, can enable a nimbler response to black swans and, of course, unplanned opportunities – such as a sudden increase in demand – which needs to be responded to effectively just as much as a disaster does.

In addition to Annex SL standards such as ISO 27001:2022, this pocket guide will also review some other risk management protocols and standards, focusing on sector-specific approaches to risk that can establish a much wider framework to risk management principles, e.g. Hazard Analysis and Critical Control Point (HACCP), which is chiefly used within food safety. In the same context, we will consider wider insights we can derive from sector-based frameworks and protocols from re approaches and there are, of course, many other frameworks and methodologies we could have taken as examples. Nevertheless, these will give a flavour of how looking at risk from a wider perspective than just one sector or approach, can inspire different and sometimes deeper or alternatives ways of identifying and controlling unplanned events. Understanding ISO 31000 can be the linchpin to this understanding.[2]

---

[2] For more information, visit: *www.iso.org/iso-31000-risk-management.html*.

CHAPTER 1: WHAT IS RISK?

Risk has many meanings and even more definitions. We will be looking at some of these in relation to management systems.

In the context of this pocket guide – which relates to management systems – the more important question is why is the idea of risk so important to the ISO 9000 family of standards? And, how can this approach help you to develop a risk-based management system?

As a starting point, ISO 9001:2015 sees risk *"as the effects of uncertainty on an expected result."*[3] ISO 31000 defines risk *"as the effects of uncertainty on objectives."*[4] Later, we will talk more about the differences between these and the definitions of risk in other standards. However, the key starting point is how the organisation views risk itself, rather than analysing how to define risk.

The ISO 9000 family of standards follows ISO's Annex SL framework (which is a relatively short document that is certainly worth reading). If we follow this framework, we have moved from simply seeing risk as the negative outcome of a probability towards seeing risk as the effects of uncertainty; this risk of uncertainty can also produce positive outcomes. For example, a better than expected order book is great, but only if we have the planning and resources in place to meet the demand – it a risk to plan for just as much as poor market performance is.

The definition of risk doesn't specifically consider countermeasures and controls. These can be defined as interventions of a temporary or permanent nature to prevent or mitigate a risk arising, or an unplanned event reoccurring. Interestingly, ISO 27001:2022 has requirements for identifying vulnerabilities, e.g. a vulnerability does not become a risk unless there is a threat to exploit it. But, how can we be aware of potential risk without considering vulnerabilities in any process,

---

[3] ISO 9001:2015.
[4] ISO 31000:2018.

whether a standard urges us to or not? It is always important to remember that Annex SL's definition of risk represents just the tip of the iceberg with regard to the layers of meaning it should provoke in terms of a strategic and tactical response to it within an organisation.

In fact, ISO has said: *"The purpose of risk management as outlined in ISO 31000 is the creation and protection of value."*[5] This idea of creating and protection of value can be seen in this broad definition of risk and opportunity that Annex SL assumes. We need a systematic approach to managing both the positive and negative risks that could compromise value (be these political, financial, ethical, technical, safety, branding, production and distribution, etc.).

Although a lot of discussion about risk is siloed, e.g. health and safety risk, financial risk, ethical risks, etc. (often with practitioners who have their own specific training and mindsets), there needs to be an overarching risk management framework. This will ensure all of these silos work towards the same ultimate objective.

One interpretation of Annex SL is that it assumes organisations are moving away from silo thinking and that risk is no different to any other process, i.e. risk management policies should sit across the organisation, and, only at tactical level do the different sector expectations come in, e.g. financial, health and safety, etc.

To consider this point from another direction we, as individuals, concern ourselves with managing uncertainty so as to protect our assets or the plans we are making for them – be that our own life or the future stock market valuation of our business. This will be peppered with many individual risks and opportunities that create or inhibit those strategic, planned outcomes occurring. In fact, many legends and popular entertainment stories are based on the quest premise – the almost impossible is eventually achieved after facing many challenges and vicissitudes, as well

---

[5] *IWA 31:2020, Risk management – Guidelines on using ISO 31000 in management systems, www.iso.org/standard/75812.html.*

as receiving unexpected help along the way. Or, in other words, the risk journey. Management systems experience such things all the time, just as we as individuals do. Risk management is fundamental to the achievement of almost all goals – so risk itself isn't the starting point – rather it is the exposure or response to the opportunity or goal being sought.

The individual propensity or desire to accept risks or pursue opportunities varies among individuals and organisations. In simplistic terms, risk-adverse organisations avoid uncertain outcomes as far as possible, devoting considerable resources to doing this. Risk takers, in contrast, will not accept that there are outcomes they cannot manage and will pursue all opportunities. Of course, most individuals fall at various points between these two extremes.

Wider societal risks – pandemics, major chemical incidents and wider political risks that go beyond the scope of the individual or an organisation – would also fall under this idea of protecting against uncertainty and, as we have seen with COVID-19, some organisations were better placed than others to manage or adapt to the ongoing, changing outcomes of the pandemic.

This risk universe isn't just an individual or one organisation, but a whole region, a nation, the world – where there are many obstacles to achieving what is planned or, sometimes, ensuring an unplanned event doesn't arise, or is at least mitigated. COVID-19 is one example of this, which, in turn, spurred on many millions of decisions relating to opportunities as well as other risks. This can also be true of ISO standards – some, such as ISO 9001, are focused very much on the individual organisation – big or small – adopting them, whereas ISO 31000 and ISO 14001 can be interpreted from an almost global perspective in terms of how the organisation interacts with interested parties.

Although some risks and opportunities can be forced upon us, others can be rejected or openly embraced – some organisations are more open to risk then others – this is called risk appetite. It is not overtly discussed in Annex SL, although it is under ISO

31000. Without understanding our risk appetite, simply defining risk is not the starting point it might otherwise appear to be.

Risk appetite is the desire, or propensity, to accept or avoid certain levels of risk in the pursuit of organisational objectives at both a strategic and tactical level. This applies to individuals, organisations (private, public and not for profit) and governments but, for brevity, we will use the term organisations.

Risk appetite needs to be distinguished from risk capacity. Risk capacity is how much risk an organisation can financially accept. This can change over time and will impact an organisation's risk appetite, i.e. all other things being equal, if the financial resources of an organisation start to diminish, then it is likely that the desire to voluntarily accept risk will be more critically examined, unless the organisation has real risk takers in that, say, the leadership team decide that one big, risky deal will solve all their immediate problems. This type of scenario reflects what is sometimes called risk tolerance – how far will an organisation stray from its usual risk appetite, i.e. almost never at all or, at the other extreme, what is risk tolerance? Again, a management system should be viewed as a tool to make sure that decisions being reached are made with the best possible management information, which will at least help the most appropriate decision to be made.

Risk appetite is influenced by risk awareness, i.e. different management teams will have a greater awareness of the vulnerabilities and risks that their organisation faces. This is one reason why the more sector-driven standards in the ISO 9000 family have much to inform those in totally different sectors, e.g. ISO 27001 with its very specific emphasis on breaking down the components of risk and the types of controls needed to address them. Arguably, if we don't understand our risk universe we can't really understand if our decisions are based on our own risk appetite or not, i.e. if we are totally unaware of a particular risk or cluster of risks in the organisation, would it change our decisions?

Was the risk-based approach to management such a significant change to the ISO 9000 family of standards?

The short answer is 'no' or, rather, management systems could always be risk-based before the risk-based approach became a requirement of the ISO 9000 family of standards.

When ISO 9001:2015 was first published, some commentators questioned why a management system needed to be risk based. The answer that emerged became clear: the Plan-Do-Check-Act Cycle (PDCA or Deming Cycle)[6] that ISO 9001 was based on can be interpreted or adapted to any risk-based approach to management. This was true even when PDCA was adopted by ISO long before any implied link to risk was referred to.

When Annex SL first adopted this risk-based approach to management, it was seen as an integral part of the PDCA. Although Deming himself focused on the reduction of waste and the promotion of teamwork, among other factors, the development of management systems wasn't yet to the level where risk and opportunities were the key drivers – we were yet to achieve consistency of outputs. But PDCA is all about making choices – resources devoted to that could be used elsewhere, e.g. business opportunities that could have been pursued but weren't. In other words, what economists call 'opportunity cost', which reflect a mixture of both risks and opportunities.

A circular process model can only work if we can move from Plan to Do to Check to Act and then feed back into the Plan element – in other words – the risk and opportunities that happen in the risk journey can be inhibitors and enablers to us achieving a consistent process of PDCA.

---

[6] W. Edwards Deming (1900–1993) was an engineer, statistician and business thinker who developed the PDCA Cycle based on the work of a fellow American, Walter A. Shewhart (1891–1967), who had developed a statistical process model that was expressed as a circular process cycle. Both the Shewhart and Deming Cycles have not only influenced Annex SL and ISO standards, but other respected approaches such as Kaizen and Lean.

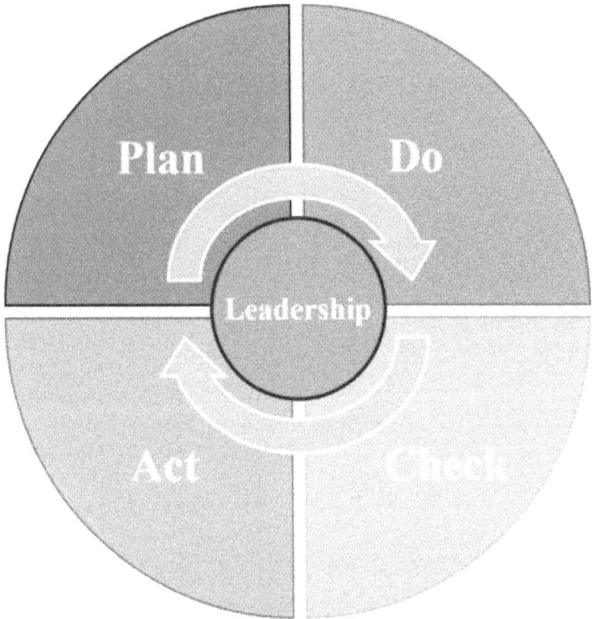

Figure 1: The PDCA cycle

It should be remembered that although PDCA seems to be a very linear reflection of processes, one can only achieve this linear progression with consistent delivery of each stage of the process – be it the highest strategic planning or assembling the cheapest component.

This is why risk, certainly in terms of ISO 31000, can be iterative as well as linear. In reality, this also applies to the ISO 9000 family of standards. The need for consistency in product delivery processes was a given long before risk and opportunities became familiar terms.

Organisations that are implementing, for example, ISO 9001 or ISO 27001 today, may express concern about a risk-based approach to management. However, we must consider that the difference between Do and Plan reflects the assessed risk and the actual outcomes to date; and Act and Check, in turn, reflects how effective we are at both identifying and controlling both actual and emerging risks, and then devising countermeasures in response to those controls that are not effective. This involves many decisions that the leadership team need to agree and implement.

This leads on to the tricky part – lots of risk-based decisions need to be made at each of the PDCA stages. These will be based on what the organisation and its stakeholders want, and how the leadership team chooses to pursue its desired goals, while maximising opportunities and mitigating risks. This is all very easy to say of course. A management system exists to provide a framework to do this and provide management information every step of the way or – to put it another way – let's go back to ISO's statement that *"the purpose of risk management is the creation and protection of value."*

In any event, the ISO 9000 family of standards isn't necessarily consistent with the way risk is defined. Some standards, such as ISO 27001:2022 (for information security management systems) and ISO 22000 (food safety management systems), define – and structure the standard itself – around a clearly understood industry expectation of risk and the response to it. Others, such as ISO 9001, are more generic in terms of being risk based, so they can apply to an extremely wide number of organisational types and sizes. In fact, it could be argued that risk management has become somewhat siloed, e.g. safety, information security and financial risk have a number of surprising communalities.

This shouldn't be seen as an inhibitor. Every organisation that wants to have an external assessment against one of these standards needs to come up with their own approach to opportunities and risk that meets their organisation's obligations, goals and priorities. This is where documents such as Annex SL and ISO 31000 can stimulate strategic thinking and practical strategies to implementing a management system that could be externally assessed.

In the process of considering all this we will also look at the lessons of other management system approaches, e.g. COBIT® 5 and CoCo which, although were defined for specific purposes, can assist in understanding how a risk-based management system can be crafted.

The purpose of the management system isn't just to provide a consistent approach to processes or even, in the worst case, a consistent bureaucracy. It should manage both opportunities and the risks that can impact upon them.

What is the risk universe?

So, rather than trying to define 'what is risk?', perhaps we should also look at the universe around this term.

The term risk universe can be interpreted in a number of ways, but in our context, it is the total number of risks an organisation – or a business or professional sector – takes or might face. This can be broken done into different silos or specialities, e.g. operational risks, financial risks, regular risks, technological risks, etc. Broadly within this definition, there is a distinction between strategic risks and those which are tactical. Equally, the distinction between risks voluntarily accepted and those that cannot be directly influenced (such as political risk or extreme weather events) can be seen. Risks that can't be influenced to the level that aligns with the risk appetite of the organisation, might suggest more resources devoted to business continuity and/or wider risk transfer mechanisms, such as insurance.

In this pocket guide, we will look at some sector-specific approaches to risk that can inform a much wider risk universe, and as explained in the Introduction, we will consider wider insights that we can derive from sector-based frameworks and protocols.

One good example concerns the risk and benefits relating to remote working. Although the main focus will be with, for example, ISO 27001 compliance, there are others risks relating to health and safety (e.g. display screen equipment regulations); there are productivity risks, impacts on teamwork and impacts on the induction of new staff members, etc. To break that down further to, for example, the use of Wi-Fi in remote locations, we have regulatory risks (such as the General Data Protection Regulation (GDPR)), productivity risks (which might be positive or negative), the greater risk of phishing attacks and the financial and technical implications of investing in a wider virtual private network (VPN). It is obvious that the decisions that need to be made here aren't simply those concerning information security, but wider risks are involved. ISO 31000 can help develop a mindset that sees these interrelationships where the circumstances might not be so obvious.

In the next chapter, we will look at ISO 31000:2018 and how this can also influence risk-based thinking (RBT) applied to the ISO 9000 family of standards.

CHAPTER 2: WHAT IS ISO 31000:2018?

In this chapter, we will look at the principles behind ISO 31000 and how these complement other approaches to risk management.

Later chapters will look at some specific ISO 31000 requirements in relation to Annex SL standards, such as ISO 9001 and ISO 27001.

It is important to show that the broad process of considering risk within ISO 31000 follows similar principles the same as many other management systems and, conversely, management systems that operate on risk-based principles can be informed by other systematic approaches to defining and controlling risk. The example we will take is HACCP, but there are a number of others we could have selected.

There is a good reason for taking this approach. The key point to remember is that, in the words of ISO itself: *"ISO 31000:2018 provides guidelines, not requirements, and is therefore not intended for certification purposes."*[7]

Sometimes the notion of a generic standard can almost be seen as a negative; after all, there are no specific requirements to understand and implement. This pocket guide is suggesting quite the opposite. Generic requirements can inform the way other more specific standards, specifications and schemes can be understood and then implemented to a greater effect. Even if you have no direct involvement with risk-based management systems outside the ISO arena, the particular examples we will discuss may inspire an alternative approach to those you already use or are thinking of adopting.

ISO defines ISO 31000 as providing:

---

[7] *ISO: The new ISO 31000 keeps risk management simple*, issued 15 February, 2018. *www.iso.org/news/ref2263.html*.

> *"Principles, a framework and a process for managing risk. It can be used by any organization regardless of its size, activity or sector."*[8]

Organisations using ISO 31000 can compare their own risk management practices with an internationally recognised benchmark. ISO goes on to say that ISO 31000 can provide *"sound principles for effective management and corporate governance."*[9]

In fact, ISO goes as far as to say:

> *"Managing risk is part of governance and leadership, and is fundamental to how the organization is managed at all levels. It contributes to the improvement of management systems."*[10]

The notion of governance is, again, implied in some Annex SL standards but is not specifically required. For example, it could be argued that ISO 9001 – despite being around in its various updates for more than 27 years – still tends to focus on effective management as meaning doing things consistently right, rather than creating processes for consistently doing right things.

Conversely, one focus of ISO 31000 is the influence of risk management on governance of the organisation. In turn, this can inspire a wider impact on policy, objectives and corrective actions through governance within an Annex SL standard, such as ISO 9001.

What are the principles behind ISO 31000?

We've already discussed that ISO 31000 looks at risk in terms of opportunities as well as negative outcomes. It also anticipates a risk management framework. Conversely, Annex SL standards expect a risk-based approach to management which, in one

---

[8] *www.iso.org/iso-31000-risk-management.html*.

[9] *www.iso.org/iso-31000-risk-management.html*.

[10] *www.iso.org/obp/ui/#iso:std:iso:31000:ed-2:v1:en*.

sense, is even more generic. This still causes confusion among some parties. ISO 31000 can help achieve a better understanding.

In the rest of this pocket guide, we will look at how ISO 31000 can inform a risk-based approach to management. However, for this chapter, we are going first to Clause 6 – the operational realisation of risk strategy and framework. This shows the tactical implications of ISO 31000, i.e. risk management is a suite of processes rather than just a principle behind it, as it might be with the ISO 9000 family of standards.

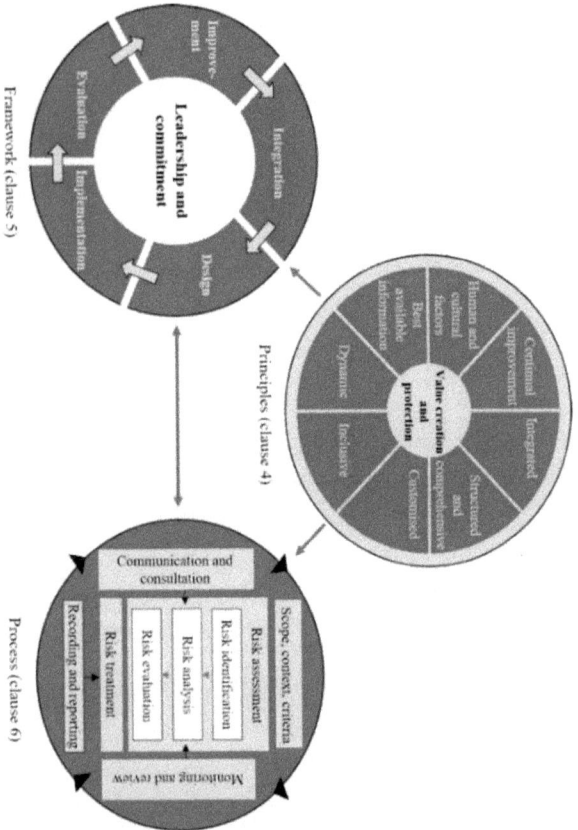

Figure 2: An adaption of ISO 31000:2018, Clauses 4, 5 and 6

We're jumping ahead to Clause 6 because this helps show that the principles of ISO 31000 have been conceived in the more practical arena of tactical, operational processes, rather than just in the areas of strategy. Also, there are many similarities in structure to the PDCA approach commonly adopted for standards such as ISO 9001 and ISO 27001. For example, Communications and Consultation, Recording and Reporting as well as Monitoring and Review.

If we go back to the ISO definition discussed earlier about providing *"principles, a framework and a process for managing risk"*, it can be seen that principles and a framework actually feed into a process. The framework that ISO 31000 creates could also be fed into existing processes, for example, ISO 9001 or ISO 27001. The framework of risk identification, risk analysis, risk evaluation and risk treatment can apply to any activity the organisation undertakes.

Although ISO 31000 isn't conceived by ISO as a standard that can be externally assessed, it could directly influence how an organisation implements other standards that can be, e.g. ISO 9001 and ISO 27001. The extent to which this would be undertaken is likely to be proportionate to the value that is being protected and the organisation's own approach to risk. This could be seen as a risk-based approach to management, which is a requirement of Annex SL standards such as ISO 9000.

It is worth looking at just one systematic approach to risk that isn't a standard and is sector specific. The one I've selected is HACCP, and how this compares with ISO 31000's Clause 6 process statement.

HACCP is always thought of in terms of food production, processing and distribution. It is, in one sense, a sequence of process controls, rather than a sequential expression of vulnerabilities and risks. However, the principles behind it follow a process methodology that is not dissimilar to ISO 31000 Clause 6. In fact, HACCP has been chosen as our first example of what a risk-based approach to management can be, simply because it defines a clear journey – or process – relating to managing risk (relating to food and beverages). Also, the ISO 9000 family of standards explicitly or implicitly requires a consistency of process or, to put it another way, to minimise variance. HACCP attempts to do this through a risk model.

HACCP is based on the notion of critical control points. Each element of any process can be broken down into stages where there will be critical control points at each stage where there is a defined standard of output. If this is not achieved, it will compromise any controls that come later in the process. It is almost like each stage of the process has its own single point of failure or, rather, failure can manifest itself later in the product production or delivery process because of a failure of controls at an earlier stage.

1. Conduct a hazard analysis

⬇

2. Determine critical control points

⬇

3. Establish critical limits

⬇

4. Establish monitoring procedures

⬇

5. Establish corrective actions

⬇

6. Establish verification procedures

⬇

7. Establish documentation procedures

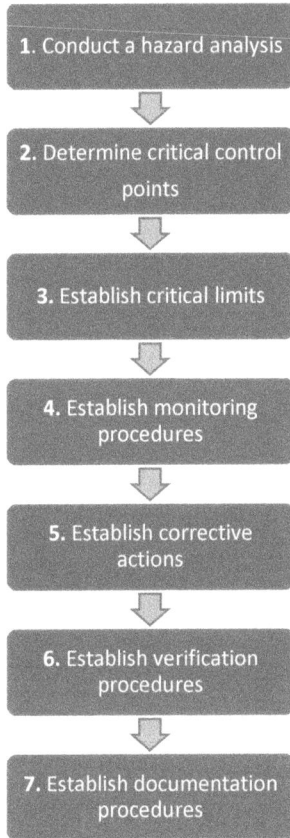

Figure 3: An adaption of the seven principles of HACCP

What ISO 31000 shows as Scope, Context and Criteria in the ISO 31000 process model can be seen as the seven stages of HACCP fleshed out as the Risk Identification, Risk Analysis and Risk Evaluation silo that sites below it. Of course, ISO 31000 addresses strategic risks as well, and these often can't be anticipated or defined like HACCP. However, there are a few wider lessons that can be discerned from this comparison.

Whether it is a strategic or tactical risk, understanding the journey or event is key. Risk identification is as much about how an unplanned event could impact an organisation and then processes defined to mitigate against this. Is this a countermeasure? Perhaps. But it is distinguished by the fact that the process – just like HACCP – is planned to be as resilient as possible so that countermeasures are not required or are not required to the same extent.

Critical points of failure are determined. In fact, when considering the risk-based approach to management required by Annex SL, defining what the key points of failure are in any process or set of processes can be very informative.

Critical points of failure can apply to many activities from design and development to managing financial ledgers. Knowing what should be done right is different to knowing what the key things are that must be right. The HACCP requirements to establishing critical limits (in simple terms, what is the distinction between acceptable or unacceptable output at that stage of a process) are another way of looking at this.

Even if the process may be seen as too complex to routinely attempt this, that is, in itself, part of the risk analysis and, later on, the risk evaluation when the effectiveness of all critical control points (and any critical limits) can be discerned. In fact, one could say Clause 6 of ISO 31000 says nothing unique – Risk Identification, Risk Analysis and Risk Evaluation can be found as concepts – if not a word for word nomenclature – in HACCP. This would also apply to most other risk-based standards and specifications.

Both ISO 31000 and Annex SL assume rational decision making – only some sectors are effective at taking into account that effective decision making – both at strategic and tactical levels – makes a significant difference to risk outcomes. One positive example would be commercial airline pilots. They spend much of their time in simulators, training on assumed scenarios and learning from their initial responses and subsequent debriefs as to what may be the best way to manage a real situation, so as to prevent or minimise an unplanned outcome. More generally, but in the same way, critical control points should make us question how far the way we assess risk and how far we look at variance in decision making are inhibitors to assuming controls will work.

At a high level, ISO 31000 and HACCP provide clear models of being aware of risk, defining it and then having management responses to it, both from strategic overviews and a more tactical response. In fact, ISO 31000 could be seen more as a strategic tool and when, in later chapters, we look at other risk frameworks, such as CoCo, we will see how such approaches can be informed by insights from ISO 31000.

Before we look in more detail at the risk-based approach to management in relation to ISO 31000 principles, we are going to consider a document that can be seen as an introduction, or glossary to ISO 31000 itself: IWA 31:2020.

CHAPTER 3: BEFORE YOU READ ISO 31000, READ THIS!

In the last chapter, we looked at how risk management principles can, actually, be very generic, even in risk-based specifications that are more sector driven, such as HACCP.

Before looking at ISO 31000 itself in more detail, we are going to consider a document that provides an overview of ISO 31000's principles and, more importantly, how they can be applied: IWA 31:2020.

Guidelines or nomenclatures to international standards sound a dull place to start. But with IWA 31:2020 it is quite the reverse. It is a goldmine of exposition as well as a reference before one reads ISO 31000 in any detail. This can also apply, to some extent, to the risk and opportunity based principles of Annex SL.

Risk management — Guidelines on using ISO 31000 in management systems[11] not only suggests specific information on how ISO 31000 can be interpreted within management systems, but also gives an example, with an imaginary business, of how ISO 31000 might be integrated into other risk-based management systems. It does this by comparing this with the ISO 31000 requirements within the high level structure (HLS) of Annex SL (pages 3-4 of IWA 31:2020). Those familiar with these documents will see this is presented in a similar way to, for example, ISO 9001:2015, where it shows how the clauses of that Standard can be aligned with other ISO standards if the organisation is integrating or combining management systems, e.g. ISO 9001 with ISO 14001.[12]

---

[11] *IWA 31:2020, Risk management – Guidelines on using ISO 31000 in management systems, www.iso.org/standard/75812.html.*

[12] A separate pocket guide on integrated management systems is available from ITGP: *Implementing an Integrated Management System (IMS) – The strategic approach* by Alan Field, www.itgovernancepublishing.co.uk/product/implementing-an-integrated-management-system-ims.

Equally, pages 3-4 of IWA 31:2020 can be used to inform how the broader risk management principles can be applied to an integrated management system and their alignment with HLS principles, which also applies to the IMS.

IWA 31:2020 explains how ISO 31000 has *"the eight principles of risk management"* and how these *"act as a foundation for the creation and protection of value."* It goes on to explain that it provides guidance on risk management systems *"communicating its value."* This can be interpreted in a number of ways, and these include the concepts of interested parties and communication and consultation, which appear in all Annex SL standards.

It is key to realise that if we see risk management as creating and protecting value, communicating what that value is and how it can be protected or nurtured is a wider concept than just compliance.

One practical example of this would be dynamic risk assessments, where people are trained to react in a risk based way, according to the circumstances presented at any given time, but only within agreed parameters. For example, don't become a victim yourself in any intervention – be it changing a leaking valve or rescuing someone from a burning building. Firefighters and mobile engineers are just two typical examples. However, it could equally apply to much wider definitions of protecting value than just matters of safety and compliance, e.g. the way business prospects are sifted for the opportunities and risks they present to the organisation. Different conflicting values may present themselves, but understanding what these values are is the starting point to identifying risk as well as controlling it. It also helps inform opportunity cost (which we will discuss later).

IWA 31:2020 also points out that *"it needs to be remembered that although the risk management process is often presented as sequential, in practice it is iterative."* This is an interesting reminder. It is often argued that Annex SL standards preach conformity. Even if this is true, it doesn't mean all processes are necessarily sequential. Some processes will require constant rework or repetition to get them to an acceptable level – this could be a design process or a new way of making something, or achieving an adequate, cost-effective repair, for example. Some textbook process models assume a sequential approach, and this can impact the effectiveness of looking at processes in a risk-based way. To counter this view, some methodologies, such as Six Sigma and Lean, directly (or sometimes indirectly) assume iterative processes, and if you are familiar with them, then this will inform your view of risk. It is always worth remembering that an unidentified vulnerability or risk could change the sequential nature of risk. This can apply to two or more process failures occurring at or near the same time that then leading to a more serious incident than the sequential nature of risk might anticipate.

Opportunities and risk lie at each cycle or stage of an iterative process, and to have a defined risk framework is one way of minimising risk. The risk to value might be opportunity cost, e.g. time being spent on further tweaks to a process that could be assigned more profitably elsewhere.

Opportunity might be seen as a standalone enhancement that strengthens an organisation's reputation or something that gives it a competitive advantage. Equally, the notion of opportunity might be seen as something that is opposite to the same coin called risk; opportunity can mitigate risk. One example of this would be the opportunities created by a new automated process that means fewer safety risks to workers as well as other potential advantages such as, perhaps, more consistent outputs. Some also view successful opportunities as paying for their failures – it is the end-of-year accounts that might reflect success, not individual entries that make them up. Whatever one's view, opportunity and risk are inextricably linked in many scenarios.

IWA 31:2020 gives a case study to explain this in practical terms. The fictional organisation 'XYZ' comes with a description of how it implemented ISO 31000 principles in its existing Annex SL management systems, chiefly focusing on ISO 9001. Even if XYZ's circumstances do not align with your organisation then, of course, principles of how decisions relating to value within their management system probably do.

There are two particular points to look at. Firstly, on page 6 of IWA 31:2020 there is an integrated policy statement for ISO 9001 and ISO 31000. Again, although some of the specifics may not apply to your organisation, it does indicate how a wider definition of risk could be utilised in other Standards , e.g. *"we are committed to managing all risk in a proactive and effective manner"*,[13] not just RBT that applies to quality objectives but all risk.

Secondly, there is a description of how individual ISO 9001 requirements can be enhanced by using ISO 31000 principles. Again, because of the HLS, at least some of this could be read in terms of ISO 14001 and ISO 27001 requirements, or the examples given could inspire greater thought, e.g. a working party or brainstorming session to see how the specific requirements of these standards might be enhanced with what the case study has outlined. For some standards, such as ISO 27001, where a number of specified controls have to be considered, this will also impact on the interpretation. As is always the case with documents such as IWA 31:2020, they should provoke discussion, debate and reflection, rather than provide any temptation simply to accept them or, conversely, to say none of these circumstances apply to us.

Also, very importantly, IWA 31:2020 states the core approach of what the Standard is about: *"ISO 31000 provides a common approach to managing any type of risk faced by an organization throughout its life."* Understanding that common approaches are more powerful than simply relying on siloed approaches to managing risk – this is a key thread throughout this pocket guide.

One interpretation of this IWA 31:2020 statement is that specialised approaches to risk management, quite rightly, operate within their specialised requirements, e.g. credit control

---

[13] ISO 31000:2018.

risks and fire safety risks are totally different but both protect value.

Or to put it another way, risk is no different to any other organisational policy or process, in that tactical management is often completely different to strategy. In other words, there needs to be an agreed strategy towards protecting and promoting value that the credit control manager and the fire safety manager (in our example) can operate their specialist requirements within. Arguably, Annex SL doesn't explicitly promote this approach – it is the risk-based, consistent suite of processes to quality management, information security management, environmental management or whatever Annex SL standard we are talking about.

The generic approach of ISO 31000 to risk is a strength to a strategy. In later chapters, we will see how ISO 31000 also contributes to strategy as well as informing the way you implement other Annex SL standards.

CHAPTER 4: USING ISO 31000 TO ASSIST RISK-BASED THINKING

In this chapter we will look more at ISO 31000 itself and how it can be used to influence RBT for any of the Annex SL standards. We have chosen ISO 27001:2022 just as one example, along with some references to ISO 9001.

Although ISO 31000 wasn't written with the express intention of directly assisting the understanding of Annex SL standards such as ISO 9001, it can certainly inspire better practice with such implementations. This is because the whole subject matter is risk and risk management, whereas with, for example, ISO 9001 or ISO 27001, RBT is just a component, albeit a very fundamental one in a whole host of other requirements.

When you read ISO 31000 – and it is worth doing – you will see the basic structure falls under a number of headings. We have already touched upon some of Clause 6 – Process. The first key heading, for our purposes, is Clause 4 – Principles.

ISO 31000 Clause 4 – Principles – starts with a key statement in terms of understanding what RBT can mean: *"The purpose of risk management is the creation and protection of value."*[14] The Clause goes on to say that risk management supports innovation and the achievement of objectives. It is worth remembering that defining and then striving to achieve objectives falls within the philosophy of all Annex SL management systems.

ISO 31000 doesn't explicitly state that it aligns with this PDCA but does, within Clause 4, refer to continual improvement (which is a key element of a circular approach to management). Also, if we move to Clause 5 Leadership, a circular approach is referred to in figure 2. So, not only do we monitor processes, but the lessons learned are integrated back into process design, which are subject to policies and priorities decided by leadership.

---

[14] ISO 31000:2018, Clause 4.

Under ISO 31000, design is seen in terms of designing a risk management process, just the same as we should be considering RBT as a fundamental element in process design in, for example, quality management. But do we always explicitly consider this? Or do we just focus on the mechanics of the process itself or the desired outputs? Even with health and safety, do we think about that as just a series of risks to assess and treat, or do we explicitly understand that the way a process is designed and delivered can create – or minimise – such risks rather than seeing risks as something that arises during the process itself? A simple example would be if we design a building that requires a lot of working at height to carry out maintenance. Wouldn't it be better to design the building to minimise the need to do any maintenance at all or, where it is necessary, for the maintenance to be done at ground level or other controlled conditions? This is something that would be considered in the UK as part of the Construction (Design and Management) Regulations 2015 (as well as the earlier The Work at Height Regulations 2005). Good design cand minimise the need to work at height, rather than simply defining controls for working at height. Although all Annex SL standards require RBT, it is worth being self-critical and thinking about how often we design our processes to minimise risk and maximise opportunities – this can apply to all sectors, services and products.

ISO 31000 encourages us to look at risk in the widest possible sense. This can include looking critically at what falls within risk controls. A practical example of this is ISO 27001, where controls over risks associated with external factors, such as natural disasters, etc. should be established. Standards can, in the simplest terms, encourage organisations to look at what the suite of processes to be risk managed actually encompasses. This is over and above the usual definition of continual improvement within the existing process sphere.

All these points lead to two key outcomes. Firstly, if ISO 31000 informs your organisation's adopted RBT, for example ISO 27001 or ISO 9001, then its thinking must also be compatible with the management system's process approach, be that PDCA or another model that leads to continual improvement. Secondly, it informs your organisation that risk appetite, risk identification and risk controls – among the other processes defined in ISO 31000 – are compatible with PDCA, which we will discuss further in the next chapter.

In any risk universe, data arising from implementing risk-based decisions should feed back into future leadership decisions about individual risks and how these impact on the wider organisation's business objectives. The process doesn't just end with looking at data and deciding, in isolation, if the risk process needs changing. A PDCA approach to risk encourages, literally, a circular process of business improvement, not just an interesting basket of problems resolved in different silos of technical decisions. Rather, it feeds into the continual process of planning and design.

ISO 31000 also refers to, under Clause 5, *"oversight bodies."* This is governance. It could be a supervisory board, a board of trustees or a regulator, etc.

It should also be remembered that although oversight bodies don't immediately appear to align with Annex SL standards, there are many similarities in principle. For example, if you have ISO 27001 or ISO 9001, not only do you have to comply with the law but you may also be a regulated business. You may have also voluntarily accepted trade or sector rules, or simply be part of a wider group of companies whose policies you have to follow and report upon. In a unionised business, there may be workforce agreements to follow. In other words, all are examples of oversight bodies, whether voluntarily accepted or imposed by law or regulation. It should be remembered that oversight bodies do not impact on existing risks but can generate new ones (i.e. risk of non-compliance to their requirements). Of course there may also be opportunities to exploit new opportunities through interaction and good practice.

We referred to this idea earlier *of "doing things consistently right"* rather than just doing things right and, of course, PDCA when properly deployed, encourages a critical review of decisions and their eventual outcome in terms of any impacts on deliverables. Process improvement can sometimes actually mean desisting from a course of action, just as much as trying to improve upon it.

Clause 6

Although we looked at Clause 6 earlier, we focused more on the outputs of risk management rather than the fundamentals they are based on (expressed earlier on in Clauses 6.1-6.4).

In fact, these sub-clauses are pretty much unique. ISO 9001 refers to risk a number of times, but doesn't explain the process of how one determines the effect of uncertainty or how to analyse the different approaches to deal with it. ISO 27001 does define information security controls and ISO 22000 is more precise on the process of risk management – just as two examples. So, Clauses 6.1 through to the end of 6.4 should be read in detail.

One of the early statements in Clause 6.1 is that *"The risk management process should be an integral part of management and decision-making."* Seemingly obvious but, of course, we have already established that it is all too easy to inadvertently silo risk as something divorced from business decision making. It goes on to discuss the impact of human behaviour and culture and, again, is an interesting departure from standards where human factors may be implied. ISO 31000 expresses the need for these to be considered. Risk is not just about statistical probabilities or process flows – human factors impact risk, the way it is controlled and the way it can evolve and emerge..

Clause 6.2 relates to Communications and Consultation. Arguably, it is a little wider than some clauses in other standards, such as ISO 9001, but one notable from this is that effective risk management is supported by ensuring all experiences and opinions are sought and outcomes communicated. Does your organisation say that risk assessment is purely a management issue? If so, considering the implications of this clause is important.

For example, control does not mean consultation is less important. For example, we can look at just one of a number of assurance methodologies in use – CoCo, which was a framework developed, back in 1992, by the Canadian Institute of Chartered Accountants (now CPA Canada). It outlines some 20 control criteria that a leadership team can use to manage company performance and improve decision making.

Although it was written for financial audit and corporate governance purposes, it has a number of interesting insights that can be applied to a much wider basket of risks, e.g. the notion of control includes ensuring that all staff understand the ethical values of the organisation and that there are no grey areas in terms of reporting lines and accountability. This notion of control relates to the way the process is designed and then operated on a day-to-day basis, and how routine outputs are verified to control standards or procedures by appropriate levels of authority. These are not only fundamental to the narrower definition of control in risk management, i.e. how we prevent a risk occurring and/or mitigate its impact if it does. CoCo also assumes wider implications, e.g. ethical awareness, agreed processes for communications and consultation with all staff. Decisions – and their ongoing impact – are part of internal control.

There is another way of visualising how internal controls (or what another framework, Committee of Sponsoring Organizations (COSO), describes as a "control environment") can help focus risk management design and communication. Consider the 114 controls required for information security management. Although on the face of it this may sound prescriptive, it allows each leadership team to define and implement these as they see fit (within the needs to meet legal, regulatory and, in some cases, industry technical requirements). All of this requires communication and consultation, as well as providing opportunities for continual improvement simply through the process of looking critically at a process and deciding how such a control is appropriate. In other words, can we do it better, can we really get it right first time and, if so, with less chance of unplanned outcomes arising?

In the next chapter we will look at the remaining elements of Clause 6, particularly risk assessment and treatment. Our discussion will move from process risks and opportunities to considering areas such as risk appetite and the wider considerations of a risk universe that Annex SL assumes is in place but might not specifically define.

CHAPTER 5: READING ISO 31000 WITHIN WIDER RISK CONCEPTS

Out last chapter looks at how ISO 31000 can be used throughout the life of an organisation and how it can be applied to any activity, including decision making at all levels. This is irrespective of what risk management methodologies are used. Later in the chapter we will look at another example, COBIT® 5.

ISO 31000's Clause 6.3 Scope, Context and Criteria is key to understanding how ISO 31000 can assist RBT because, unlike Annex SL, it gives a detailed breakdown of how the risk process can be seen.

Clause 6.3 includes requirements to what it calls 'risk criteria' but is often known by the term 'risk appetite'. I referred to this in Chapter 4, but understanding what this means in your own organisation brings much clarity to questions such as what risks and opportunities should be in your objectives. Understanding risk appetite will also lead to a greater understanding of why risk controls need to be in place or, rather, how their implementation should be prioritised. This equally applies to risk registers as well as objectives for quality, health and safety, anti-bribery, etc. Even with regulatory risks it isn't the done deal it might seem – risk criteria (perhaps the better term here) is equally true – do we comply, if so, how or do we want to exceed requirements? It will all be based on how far you want to accept or avoid risk and, perhaps, whether you see regulation as a cage or an opportunity.

Firstly, Clause 6.3 talks about defining the scope of the risk management process, relevant objectives to be considered and their alignment with organisational objectives. Interestingly, it talks about agreeing on the appropriate risk assessment tools and techniques as part of the scope. This is key for deciding and implementing RBT for any Annex SL standards, but it is not specifically stated. There is also reference to internal and external contexts, e.g. risk and the response to it may be influenced by internal, organisational factors as much as external factors. Organisational factors can be a source of risk and the *"purpose and scope of the risk management process may be interrelated with the objectives of the organization as a whole."*[15] Again, partially implied within Annex SL, but stated here in a more explicit and logical way, which may influence the way you see RBT.

Clause 6.3.4 Risk Criteria states that *"The organization should specify the amount and type of risk that it may or may not take, relative to objectives."*[16] In other words, consideration of the risk appetite.

One interpretation of Annex SL is that it sees risk and opportunities as being the responsibility of top management in relation to legal, contractual and the expectations of interested parties. However, the amount of risk each organisation is prepared to accept – sometimes seen as a simplistic binary idea of risk takers and those who are more cautious, will in reality be more of a mixture of both, with certain business processes being managed more conservatively than others. Risk appetite can be based on resources – a multinational corporation may have the financial resources to take risks in certain areas, whereas a small business probably can't. Individual boards of directors may have a groupthink that is more cautious or, alternatively more swashbuckling.

Before we define risk and opportunities, we need to consider why we have chosen to ignore or downgrade some risks in relation to others, and why we want to exploit some opportunities and ignore others – the latter case is often because of caution over resources being devoted to something that may prove to be a failure, or simply a road we don't want to travel down. But explicit discussion about risk appetite is not always on a risk agenda. This is a pity because risk appetite is really a form of strategic thinking – a board needs to understand why

---

[15] ISO 31000:2018.
[16] ISO 31000:2018.

there are risks and opportunities they simply don't want to be exposed to (or actively pursue) at any given time.

Your risk appetite isn't set in stone – new circumstances as well as new members of a leadership team can lead to change, so there should be a periodic review to consider attitudes to how much risk and how many different opportunities should be actioned.

One way of looking at how both risk appetite and the way risk is identified – particularly in terms of management systems applications such as the ISO 9001 family of standards – would look at how strategic and tactical decisions are made and reviewed.

The risk assessment section, Clause 6.4, gives a detailed breakdown of the stages of risk assessment, something that Annex SL doesn't do. For example, with ISO 9001, the focus of RBT is risk and opportunities based Quality Objectives but there is little guidance within the Standard itself to define any framework to do this. However, when we look at IS0 31000, the generic nature of the processes shown in Clause 6.4 can provide an approach.

Let's look at one common example, the risk of customer dissatisfaction, e.g. we identify that customer perception is a risk to the organisation's value (it could be financial, brand, reputational, etc.). Then, through further analysis – such as examining the results of a customer survey – we might set a target for improvement. This can be defined as a Quality Objective. Clause 6.4.2 of ISO 31000 says: *"The purpose of risk identification is to find, recognise and describe risks that might help or prevent an organization achieving its objectives."* But equally, an Objective can define or justify resources being devoted to preventing or inhibiting an incident or series of incidents arising from less than adequate customer satisfaction, e.g. customers going elsewhere, product returns eating into profits, etc.. In our example, the treatment of the risk is the way either we improve customer satisfaction results and, depending on the reasons, the methods for achieving a desired result are defined and monitored.

The stages suggested follow a process but, of course, processes aren't always linear, i.e. defining risks and opportunities can be iterative, e.g. risks can emerge suddenly and the decisions on treatment options need to be equally nimble. For example, an unexpected legal dispute or a sudden upturn in business are both risks and opportunities to treat to ensure unplanned outcomes don't spiral out of control. Annex SL looks at risk in a greater horizon scan – certification bodies typically use an annual cycle in terms of expecting Objectives to be reviewed, although an organisation can (and should) review risk and opportunities based Objectives more regularly if circumstances dictate.

If we use Clause 6 of ISO 31000 to inspire a different way of looking at how our risk and opportunities based management system works, is this more than just a matter of risk? In other words, are there other structural changes that would make this simpler to do?

As just one example, a framework conceived for the IT sector that might be interpreted for a wider range of processes is COBIT® 5. (It should be remembered there is at least one other version of COBIT® available but we have taken 5 for the purpose of our discussion.)

COBIT® 5 helps organisations meet business challenges in the areas of regulatory compliance, risk management and aligning IT strategy with organisational goals.

Although this is an IT-focused framework – just like HACCP for the food sector we considered earlier – the general principles of COBIT® 5 can certainly inform a risk-based framework for managing different types of business risk.

COBIT® 5 is based on five principles that are essential for the effective management and governance of enterprise IT:

1. **Principle 1:** Meeting stakeholder needs
2. **Principle 2:** Covering the enterprise end to end

3. **Principle 3:** Applying a single integrated framework
4. **Principle 4:** Enabling a holistic approach
5. **Principle 5:** Separating governance from management

These five principles enable an organisation to build a holistic framework for the governance and management of IT that is built on seven 'enablers':

1. **People, policies and frameworks**
2. **Processes**
3. **Organisational structures**
4. **Culture, ethics and behaviour**
5. **Information**
6. **Services, infrastructure and applications**
7. **People, skills and competencies**

Together, the principles and enablers allow an organisation to align its IT investments with its objectives to realise the value of those investments.

Although the detail of these enablers is different to the ISO 9001 family of standards, you can see the broad similarities that mean the structure can be adapted to a risk and opportunity approach to management, e.g. emphasis on processes; culture, ethic and behaviour; people, skills and competencies, etc. There are also clearly delineated roles for governance and management, which can be adapted to include the way the governance function(s) can set a high level policy towards risk and the reporting function from management as to how risks, opportunities and controls are operating in practice and in light of dynamic circumstances.

Secondly, with COBIT® 5 there is an emphasis on end-to-end enterprise thinking – with risk management this would mean considering risks and opportunities to value from the very beginning of the process to any post-delivery activities, e.g. servicing. What might seem a good control for one part of the process could create issues elsewhere in the pipeline, i.e. the holistic principles of COBIT® 5 would align well. This can be a bit like HACCP – with its critical control points – which are all individually important but, equally, can't be considered in isolation. End-to-end thinking is a risk control in itself, and the time and money invested in it reflects as much the current appetite for risk, as much as meeting any specific framework requirements.

To help conceptualise this, when COBIT® 5 was reissued as COBIT® 2019, the term 'enablers' was renamed 'components', among other changes. In its wider meaning, components make up a working device. In a risk management process, components can be seen as parts of the risk universe that needs integration and maintenance in design, operation and review. Or, to put it another way, thought and planning into design, operation and review – a management system and not just a risk management system. In RBT, consider that the T word – thinking – is arguably an important one.

Whether you are using Monte Carlo simulations or simply tossing a dice, both are a reflection of risk appetite. Of course, the tools chosen to assess and control risk are the topic of another book. One important point to consider is that ISO 31000 makes us realise how important the evaluation of the risk tools and techniques selected is, along with monitoring and measurement techniques to analyse outcomes, expected or otherwise.

Many organisations can define RBT for an Annex SL standard with relatively few complexities – whereas other equally effective leadership teams find the process a challenge. This might be caused by divorcing RBT from their Objectives or, perhaps, seeing their outcomes as not representing risk or opportunities but as simply an output, whether it was desired or otherwise. It might also be because risk appetite has never been explicitly discussed or factored in. Some organisations, for regulatory or market reasons, are tied to a particular risk management approach or expectation, and are not necessarily looking for inspiration from how other sectors may see risk and its management differently. Equally, some organisations think the process cycle(s) they use to deliver to their customer base must follow a particular method of risk-based controls, and other approaches would not assist their continual improvement. This pocket guide has aimed to show how this is not necessarily the case and how looking at even quite specific elements of ISO 31000 can inspire a better understanding of RBT, and how this can lead to a more enhanced approach to any Annex SL standard you have implemented or plan to implement.

CONCLUSION

We have seen how RBT is a key component to understanding Annex SL based standards, and to understand what RBT actually means to individual organisations is influenced very much by the risk appetite of individual leadership teams and to, a certain extent, by market and regulatory expectations that impact on their strategic visions.

In one sense, ISO 31000 provides a strategic overview of the risk management universe but can impact on RBT at a more tactical level, e.g. the way we can better prioritise competing risk controls based on the way we now understand our risk appetite, rather than just the perceived risk rankings themselves. The importance of this realisation is that, in many cases, the risk profile will be too wide ranging to be given an equal priority for treatment; understanding appetite and any limitations of individual risk controls is key to minimising any unplanned events arising.

ISO 31000, read in conjunction with Annex SL, makes the notion of risk wider than just negative, unplanned events. The simplistic model of risk versus benefits can apply to opportunities and improvement – investment decisions on new products are influenced by risk appetite just as much as managing fire risks or credit risks, for example. Managing risk is just as much about opportunity than anything negative – if an organisation can promote this realisation, then cooperation with the risk management process will be galvanised.

FURTHER READING

IT Governance Publishing (ITGP) is the world's leading publisher for governance and compliance. Our industry-leading pocket guides, books, training resources and toolkits are written by real-world practitioners and thought leaders. They are used globally by audiences of all levels, from students to C-suite executives.

Our high-quality publications cover all IT governance, risk and compliance frameworks and are available in a range of formats. This ensures our customers can access the information they need in the way they need it.

Other publications by Alan Field include:

- *Implementing an Integrated Management System (IMS) – The strategic approach*,
  www.itgovernancepublishing.co.uk/product/implementing-an-integrated-management-system-ims
- *ISO 50001 – A strategic guide to establishing an energy management system*,
  www.itgovernancepublishing.co.uk/product/iso-50001
- *ISO 37001 – An Introduction to Anti-Bribery Management Systems*,
  www.itgovernancepublishing.co.uk/product/iso-37001

For more information on ITGP and branded publishing services, and to view our full list of publications, visit *www.itgovernancepublishing.co.uk*.

To receive regular updates from ITGP, including information on new publications in your area(s) of interest, sign up for our newsletter at:
www.itgovernancepublishing.co.uk/topic/newsletter.

Further reading

Branded publishing

Through our branded publishing service, you can customise ITGP publications with your company's branding.

Find out more at:
www.itgovernancepublishing.co.uk/topic/branded-publishing-services.

Related services

ITGP is part of GRC International Group, which offers a comprehensive range of complementary products and services to help organisations meet their objectives.

For a full range of resources on risk management visit *www.itgovernance.co.uk/shop/category/risk-management-frameworks*.

Training services

The IT Governance training programme is built on our extensive practical experience designing and implementing management systems based on ISO standards, best practice and regulations.

Our courses help attendees develop practical skills and comply with contractual and regulatory requirements. They also support career development via recognised qualifications.

Learn more about our training courses in risk management and view the full course catalogue at *www.itgovernance.co.uk/training*.

Professional services and consultancy

We are a leading global consultancy of IT governance, risk management and compliance solutions. We advise businesses around the world on their most critical issues and present cost-saving and risk-reducing solutions based on international best practice and frameworks.

We offer a wide range of delivery methods to suit all budgets, timescales and preferred project approaches.

Further reading

Find out how our consultancy services can help your organisation at *www.itgovernance.co.uk/consulting*.

Industry news

Want to stay up to date with the latest developments and resources in the IT governance and compliance market? Subscribe to our Weekly Round-up newsletter and we will send you mobile-friendly emails with fresh news and features about your preferred areas of interest, as well as unmissable offers and free resources to help you successfully start your projects. *www.itgovernance.co.uk/weekly-round-up*.

EU for product safety is Stephen Evans, The Mill Enterprise Hub, Stagreenan, Drogheda, Co. Louth, A92 CD3D, Ireland. (servicecentre@itgovernance.eu)

www.ingramcontent.com/pod-product-compliance
Lightning Source LLC
Chambersburg PA
CBHW042119190326
41519CB00030B/7548